D1593474

Speed Training
for
Martial Arts and
MMA

How to Maximize Your Hand Speed,
Boxing Speed, Kick Speed and Power,
Punching Speed and Power, plus
Wrestling Speed and Power for
Combat and Self-Defense

J. Barnes

Focus on Solutions®

ISBN: 0-9768998-0-9

Library of Congress Control Number:
2005928718

Cover Designer Michael Cox
Managing Editor Linda Cole

Produced in the United States of America

J. Barnes has more than 20 years of experience in Mixed Martial Arts. He coined the term "Speed Loop™" and just recently agreed to reveal the details of his innovative speed training system in this exclusive publication for Fitness Lifestyle.

Disclaimer

(Please Read Carefully!)

Please note that the author and/or publisher of this instructional guide are NOT RESPONSIBLE in any manner whatsoever for any injury that may occur by reading and/or following the instructions herein.

The author and/or publisher are not responsible for any injury to anyone who utilizes the information contained within this guide or to anyone injured due to the actions of one who utilizes the information contained herein.

The author and/or publisher advocate responsible behavior in all cases, and in no way endorse or condone street fighting, illegal behavior or unprovoked violent actions.

It is absolutely essential that before following any of the activities, physical or otherwise, described herein, the reader should first consult his or her physician for advice on whether to embark on the activities, physical or otherwise, described herein.

Since the physical and/or psychological activities described herein may be too sophisticated in nature for the untrained person, *it is absolutely essential that a physician be consulted prior to their implementation.*

Dedication

I would first and foremost like to dedicate this guide to Clarence W. Hawkins, for giving me my first martial arts book. It is from that book that I got the initial spark which has resulted in the publication of this guide.

Secondly, I would like to dedicate this guide to all of you who are committed to the necessary evolution of martial arts.

Acknowledgments

Special thanks to the following for their contributions: Terrance "Tank" Tobias, Steven Elder, the late Brian Fletcher, David L. Jones, Maurice "June" Wilkens, the late Larry "Quiet Man" Marks, Linda D. Jones, Joseph L. Jones, Michael L. Jones, Marcia B. Goffney, Anitra C. Marsh, Steven M. Marsh, the late Fatimah, Joseph Jones Jr., and the late Evelyn L. Jones.

— J. Barnes

Contents

Getting Started

I have written this guide with a single objective in mind: to help you become a superior fighter by increasing your speed to the highest level of your innate potential.

Speed is a key attribute for success in competition and self-defense. Reaction speed is often the sole difference between winning and losing a physical confrontation.

Regardless of your fighting style or method— you cannot apply it unless you can react quickly and respond accurately! That is exactly what this guide will teach you how to do.

I have heard about countless people who have enrolled in martial arts schools and trained diligently for months or even years, only to find their so-called "deadly techniques" have failed to save them in a real fighting situation.

What went wrong? Why didn't their techniques work as they did in class? Could this happen to you? You bet it could—unless you shift your focus from demonstrations and controlled sparring and start focusing on success in competition and self-defense.

After reading this guide, you will know how to train effectively. You will not be seduced by an instructor's board breaking demonstration. You will not even be impressed with an instructor who can throw 20 punches in one second! You—the informed speed student—will know that such demonstrations have little, if anything, to do with speed in competition and self-defense.

The essential ingredient, which I have found all superior fighters possess, is the ability to instantly separate the useful from the useless. By doing so, they are able to get much more out of their training and achieve high levels of skill much faster.

What You Will Find in This Guide

This book is divided into 10 chapters. The following is a brief description of the contents of each.

Chapter 1: The Speed Loop™

You will receive the facts on the Speed Loop™ and its seven vital components.

Chapter 2: Visual Reflexes

This chapter contains the training methods that will increase your visual reflexes for spotting openings and tracking movements. You will need these reflexes primarily for long-range fighting.

Chapter 3: Tactile Reflexes

This is an examination of methods that will develop your tactile (touch) reflexes. You will learn to anticipate an opponent's every move while you are in the trapping or grappling range. Almost all fights end up in this range. Be prepared!

Chapter 4: Auditory Reflexes

Focus on training your auditory reflexes by improving your listening skills. If you have ever experienced blind fighting, or fighting in the dark, you won't dispute the importance of this attribute!

Chapter 5: Adaptation Speed

Focus on improving your mind's ability to instantaneously select the perfect action in response to an attack or opening. You will learn to respond accurately without thought.

Chapter 6: Initiation Speed

This chapter will cover the critical development of your explosiveness, once you have chosen the correct action to initiate. You will learn to make your movements felt before they are seen.

Chapter 7: Movement Speed

You will learn to develop the only speed that is recognized by the public at large—movement speed. You will not use it for demonstration purposes. You will use movement speed to overwhelm and subdue an opponent in seconds!

Chapter 8: Alteration Speed

You will be introduced to the "safeguard," known as alteration speed. Through mastery of body mechanics, you will develop the ability to stop instantly in the midst of movement—just in case you initiate a wrong move!

Chapter 9: Speed Hampering

Review the latest techniques on speed hampering. After covering this chapter, you will understand exactly how to immobilize, confuse, and ultimately, destroy your opponent's confidence and ability to harm you.

Chapter 10: Supplemental Speed Training

Now you can enhance your speed using supplemental speed training. You will learn how to get that extra edge that often separates the superior fighter from the average fighter.

How to Get Your Money's Worth from This Book

You should not just read this guide and put it aside once you are done. I am your consultant, and this guide constitutes an active conversation between two people: you, who want to become a superior fighter by maximizing your total speed, and me, who have presented the essential information that will enable you to achieve your goal.

You can rest assured that this guide is unlike any other ever published on developing speed for competition and self-defense. It will echo the realities of speed training for martial arts as they stand today. If applied correctly, the guidance provided will double or triple your speed.

You must give effort before you get results. Open your mind to the teachings and implement them on a deliberate and consistent basis. This is the only way to improve. It will not happen by accident.

All superior fighters have come to the realization that they are their own worst enemy.

The most difficult aspect of transforming your body in any way is the task of first transforming your mind and emotions. That will lead to the physical transformation you desire.

I suggest you glance through the guide once to get a conceptual view of its contents and direction. From there, you should study one chapter at a time. The chapters are in specific order as they come into play in the Speed Loop™.

You are a unique individual and should be treated as such. Therefore, you should read this guide at a pace that is effective for you.

After capturing the essence of each chapter, you can then proceed by trying the specific drills. Taking these steps in order will prevent you from wasting your valuable training time. Superior fighters do not waste training time!

You will get the most from this guide, or any other, by continuously following these five steps:

1. Know your definite purpose or goal.
2. With an open mind, study the material thoroughly.
3. Grasp everything that is beneficial to your purpose or goal.

4. Release everything that is useless to your purpose or goal.

5. Apply the modified outcome on a focused and consistent basis to realize your purpose or goal in the shortest possible time.

A Few Words about Me and My Role in Your Life

I have studied martial arts for more than 20 years. During those years, I have gone through many physical and mental transformations. Every one of those transformations has been for the better, because I am constantly striving to improve my knowledge, awareness, and effectiveness.

I grew up spending a lot of time on rough city streets, which led to me being in real streetfights. I have studied many forms of martial arts, and I know which styles are best suited for self-defense—and why.

As a young boy, I was nicknamed "Rabbit" by my older brother Joseph, because he said I was fast like a rabbit. In order to realize my full speed potential, I devoured all the information on speed training I could get my hands on. From there, I tested and developed those methods to ensure effectiveness. The results are contained within this guide.

In this guide, you will find the truth about developing your speed attributes for competition and self-defense. I will not mislead you regarding what it really takes to maximize your speed. A lot of people out there will. Do not let them!

If you ever have any questions about improving your speed training, feel free to send them to me through the publisher. I will do my best to provide you with the truth, in the form of a reply, or possibly an entirely new guide, written by me or another authority on the subject. Fair enough?

Okay, enough about that—now let's get started on your speed training.

Secret: The quickest and most effective way to improve your total speed is to frequently train with someone in whom these attributes function at a higher level than in yourself. In other words— you will get faster by training with someone who is faster than you!

Chapter 1

The Speed Loop™

The Speed Loop™ is comprised of the seven components of speed and their relation to each other when applied in competition or self-defense. As a speed student, it is imperative that you thoroughly understand the Speed Loop™.

This chapter will introduce you to vital theories of total martial arts speed. You will learn about successful advanced speed training concepts. You will also learn about the useless concepts that you should abandon in competition and self-defense.

Secret: You should focus on the maximum development of each individual Speed Loop™ component. By doing this, you will train more effectively and achieve superior combat speed in the shortest possible time.

Applied Speed vs. Demonstration Speed

Before you learn about successful speed training concepts, I need to first bring to your attention some speed myths that might be somewhat confusing.

Can you really hit a person 20 times in one second? Well, let's see. It depends on the distance from your hands to the target. If your hands are just one inch from the target, then it might be possible—in theory.

But, if you are attempting to throw 20 fully extended and retracted punches from your chest in one second—forget it! I am 6'1" tall, with long arms. I can't possibly pull that stunt off. The truth is, nobody can!

Now let's add the factor of realistic fighting. Ask yourself: What kind of damage can 20 lightning-quick punches do in one second from a one-inch distance? You would be moving so fast that your punches would look like one blur—an impressive demonstration for sure!

In a physically threatening confrontation, I would much prefer to throw one explosive and destructive finger jab through the eyes than to throw 20 light taps to the body. Which tactic is more likely to stop an attacker?

For another comparison, you have probably scen movies in which a martial artist wielded a pair of nunchukas. When demonstrated by a trained weapons person, these flashy tools can give the impression of supernatural speed.

Most novices, unfamiliar with using weapons in martial arts, view this as real speed. It is demonstration speed—*not* applied speed.

Simply ask anyone who understands the benefits and limits of weapons in combat. They will choose a plain stick over the nunchuka every time. The nunchuka appears more impressive, but the stick *performs* better for self-defense purposes.

What are the odds that you will spot a pair of nunchukas lying on the ground if you are attacked on the street? Not very good. Maybe you won't find a stick either. But what you should do is *utilize what is readily available* in order to defend yourself. Use whatever you can get your hands on!

Applied speed in fighting is much more intricate than a simple demonstration. The variables and intensity levels are not comparable.

Do not be seduced by outlandish claims regarding the effectiveness of a particular style or weapon. It is the individual who determines the effectiveness of the style or weapon. Ultimately, the level of your attributes, knowledge, and experience against that of your opponent will determine your success in competition and self-defense.

C.C.S. Principle

As a speed student, you must make consistent use of the C.C.S. principle: *Combat Common Sense!*

Combat Common Sense must take precedence over theoretical notions. In theory, it would seem that a trained black belt in Karate could easily defeat an unschooled street thug. Combat

Common Sense will tell you this notion is not necessarily true.

Do not believe in theories until you have successfully applied them in realistic training. When you fully believe in a concept and understand how it works, you can apply that concept decisively, in the midst of combat, without second-guessing its validity.

Do not ignore your common sense! Use it as a finely tuned scam detector. The more adept you are at avoiding spurious myths, the more easily you will hone in on the essential concepts that will accelerate your improvements in speed movement.

Be truthful with yourself concerning the strengths and weaknesses in your Speed Loop™. Most people concentrate too much on their strongest components, to the detriment of other, underdeveloped ones. This is one of the biggest mistakes made by beginning students. But this will not be you! You will develop a strong and balanced Speed Loop™!

In order to improve consistently and continuously, you must vigorously search for any weaknesses in your loop that need immediate attention and development. At the same time, you must maintain your strongest components.

Remember: Your Speed Loop™ is only as strong as its weakest individual component!

Isolation Principle

The isolation principle is used to make rapid progress in each Speed Loop™ component, thereby achieving maximum total speed improvement in the shortest possible time.

Using the isolation principle requires that you totally involve yourself with "here and now." This is where your absolute power lies. Do not concern yourself with "there and then," which deals with false perceptions of power.

You should maintain this sense of purpose, in the present, throughout every phase of every training session. Here are some other key points on isolation training:

- Begin by clearing your mind and reviewing the exact component(s) you will be training, prior to beginning any exercise drill.

- Be willing to concentrate intensely on developing that component by giving it your total, undivided attention.

- Be certain to train where and when you will not be disturbed unless there is an emergency.

- For speed purposes, realize that five minutes of intense component training is more productive than fifteen minutes of lackadaisical component training.

Secret: The more you can break down an attribute in training, the more productive your training will be. That is the purpose of the Speed Loop™. It provides a vehicle through which you can effectively use the parts of the whole to make a significant and rapid impact on the whole. As your Speed Loop™ components improve, your total speed will improve dramatically.

Chapter 2

Visual Reflexes

This chapter will decrease your reaction time to visual stimuli in fighting. For defensive purposes, you will learn to anticipate, recognize, and track swift movements. For offensive purposes, you will learn to quickly spot openings and opportunities to attack.

Developing speed in visual recognition and tracking is a main foundation for the speed student. If you lack tremendous movement speed, you can compensate for this weakness through quick seeing. Great visual reflexes are rarely inherited. They are usually the result of conscious and consistent development.

Eye Exercises

You should begin your visual reflexes training by exercising your eyes. Like any other muscle, the eye muscles need to be warmed up and prepared for more demanding work. This will help to ensure maximum functioning of your visual reflexes. Here are the recommended exercises for stretching, strengthening, and relaxing your eyes.

Lateral Eye Stretch

Sit in a relaxed position. Look straight ahead. Without moving your head, look as far to your right as you can. You should feel a slight stretch in your eye muscles. Hold the stretch for five seconds. Now focus your eyes straight ahead, relaxing them for one second. Repeat the eye stretch to your left, without moving your head. Hold for five seconds. Again, focus straight ahead and relax the eyes for one second. That is one repetition. You should do 10-20 repetitions.

Vertical Eye Stretch

Sit in a relaxed position. Look straight ahead. Without moving your head, look as far down as you can. You should feel a slight stretch in your eye muscles. Hold the stretch for five seconds. Now focus your eyes straight ahead, relaxing them for one second. Repeat the eye stretch looking as far upward as you can, without moving your head. Hold for five seconds. Again, focus straight ahead and relax the eyes for one second. That is one repetition. You should do 10-20 repetitions.

Circular Eye Stretch

Sit in a comfortable position. Look straight ahead. Visualize a large clock, about 10 feet in diameter, directly in front of your face. Imagine your nose is fixed to the center of the clock.

Looking up, fix your sight first on the clock's 12. Moving your eyes clockwise, fix your sight on the 1. Keep moving your eyes clockwise, stopping at each number, until you go all the way around to 12 again. Rest the eyes for a few seconds. Repeat this exercise going counter-clockwise.

During the circular eye stretch, it is important to pause your focus briefly at each number on the imaginary clock. It is also important that you stretch your eye muscles to see each number. Remember: the clock is 10 feet across.

Eye Squeeze

Sit in a comfortable position. Look straight ahead. Now squeeze your eyes shut tightly. Hold the eye squeeze for five seconds. Open your eyes and relax them briefly before repeating the eye squeeze. You should do 5-10 repetitions.

Eye Massage

Sit in a comfortable position. Allow your head to gently fall forward, as if you are falling asleep. Close your eyes and relax all of your facial muscles. Begin to gently massage the lids of your closed eyes with your fingers using the following techniques:

1. Downward stroke: slide the fingers from the eyebrows down to the cheekbones while applying slight pressure as the fingers first contact the eyelids.

2. Outward stroke: slide the fingers from the bridge of the nose out to the temples while applying slight pressure as the fingers make contact with the eyelids.

Warning: The eye is a very delicate organ. I strongly advise you to proceed with caution when practicing these eye exercises. You must be careful not to strain the eye or the eye muscles. Be careful to avoid pushing too hard on your eyelids.

Blink Control

Crucial to "quick seeing" is the ability to control the natural tendency to blink. All superior full-contact fighters have learned blink control—consciously or unconsciously. Blink control will ensure maximum use of your visual reflexes. Being able to resist closing the eyes during a fight can mean the difference between victory and being pummeled by your adversary. If you can't "see" it, you will surely "feel" it when it gets there!

We all blink naturally. This natural blinking happens in a microsecond and cannot be eliminated. What I am talking about is eliminating the habit of closing your eyes when you are attacked. Developing blink control is more of a psychological task than a physical one.

Closing your eyes in the midst of fighting reduces your chances of success. I realize there are exceptions to every rule. For instance, it would make sense to close your eyes if someone hurled a handful of sand toward your eyes. The goal is not to have your eyes closed any longer than they absolutely need to be.

The following are the recommended drills for developing blink control.

Blink Challenge

You will need someone to help you with this drill. Start by standing with your hands at your side. Have your training partner stand about five feet in front of you. Your partner should now attempt to find your "blink point." How close to your eyes does an attack have to be to make you blink? Your partner's goal is to make you blink. Your goal is not to blink. It's that simple. Some people can easily be made to blink. Some superior fighters do not seem to blink even when they are hit.

First, your partner could try stomping or yelling abruptly. If that doesn't work, your partner could try punches or kicks launched toward your face.

Your partner should not come too close until you can control your response. As you gain control over your blinking, have your partner throw punches and kicks that come within an inch of your face. Be sure your partner can accurately judge the distance between you. In addition, I strongly recommend that you wear protective headgear to avoid injury when practicing these drills. You will probably feel the wind from these attacks, but just concentrate on relaxing and not blinking.

The last step is to have your partner put on boxing gloves and footpads. Your partner should now make very light contact. Do not concern yourself with defense at this time. Just focus on controlling your blinking. Once you can handle this, try some fast light-contact sparring. This will help you develop blink control.

Do not go all out when sparring for blink control. Emphasize fast, yet light, contact. You should each try to get the other to close his or her eyes by using feints and broken rhythm. Focus on the goal of the training: to develop blink control. You should always have a purpose and focus for every training drill or exercise. This will allow you to achieve the desired results much faster.

Peripheral Vision

Your visual reflexes can be improved immediately if you learn to diffuse your vision. Reaction speed is affected by the distribution of the observer's attention. Fewer separate choices lead to faster actions. Many separate choices lead to slower actions.

Visual reflexes operate best when your awareness shifts from small details to larger ones, and finally to the whole action, without a thought being given to any single part. This allows you to react quickly without excessive lag time between stimulus and response.

Get into the habit of observing everything around you. Do not study it—just relax and be aware of its movement. Detachment of the mind is the key here, though a focus point is needed to ensure maximum concentration.

The following drills are designed to improve your peripheral vision.

Public Awareness

Focus your eyes on a distant structure, such as a high building or pole. Now diffuse your vision. You should be able to see the structure clearly, and also the blurry environment bordering it. You might see people, cars, or other objects. Take note of any movement from both corners of your eyes. Try to really see what is going on around you while your eyes are fixated on the focus structure.

Name Call

Enlist the help of three or more training partners and spread them out in a line facing you. Stand about 10 feet in front of them. Now focus on all of them by diffusing your vision. Your eyes focus on the person in the middle, but your peripheral vision is actually upon the outer two at the same time. As one of them moves any body part, no matter how slightly, call out the person's name.

> **Secret:** You can practice sparring with two or more people as your peripheral vision improves. This is the best way to improve your peripheral vision for competition and self-defense purposes.

Alphabet Game

Stand about 15 feet in front of your training partner. Have your training partner draw imaginary letters of the alphabet in the air with a finger as you attempt to distinguish the letters. To make this more of a challenge, have your partner move to the right or left so as to be out of your direct view. Have your partner speed up, slow down, and break rhythm while drawing letters. You must keep your drills consistently challenging if you seek rapid improvement.

Visual Stamina

Visual stamina involves the ability to quickly focus on an object. It also involves the ability to concentrate intensely on that object for a prolonged period of time. The development of your visual stamina will enable you to experience the sensation of "speed-retardation." This is when the fastest punch or kick appears to be moving in slow motion.

Understand this: A punch or kick is as fast as it appears to the person viewing it. To the untrained eye, a movement may appear to be very fast. On the other hand, that same movement may appear quite slow to the trained eyes of an advanced speed student.

You have probably already experienced the "speed-retardation" phenomenon. It usually occurs during an extremely stressful situation, and it can happen in seconds. First, the adrenaline rush kicks in. Then your eyes bulge, and your heart will begin to beat faster. You might get butterflies in your stomach. In this particular state of mind, humans are capable of lifting cars, absorbing great punishment, and a host of other seemingly "amazing" physical feats.

When we examine the adrenaline rush a little closer, we find that the key difference resulting from this state, as compared to a relaxed state, is intense concentration. During the adrenaline rush, you are absolutely and totally focused on the task at hand. Your body automatically pushes your concentration powers into overdrive. This eliminates every mental distraction and allows you to make maximum use of your physical capabilities.

You should not wait until you experience a real-life combat situation to start making use of the adrenaline rush as a training tool. Instead, you must learn to consciously release the adrenaline rush by improving your ability to focus and concentrate.

There are two steps to mastering the adrenaline rush. Step one is to develop the ability to *release* it. Step two is to develop the often-overlooked ability to *control* it.

As a serious speed student, your goal is to reach the point where you can cut the adrenaline rush on and off at will. This is an essential skill for competition and self-defense.

Secret: I believe the control and use of the adrenaline rush is, in fact, the same inner power that is known in martial arts circles as Ki or Chi.

To instantly turn your Ki on, try this: Open your eyes as wide as you can. Begin taking slow and deep breaths. Now relax and concentrate on the energy flowing through your body. Try to really feel the energy. It's just the oxygen that you're breathing in. It is oxygen that fuels the adrenal response.

Next, speed up your breathing as fast as you can, still breathing very deeply. Conjure up feelings of extreme fear or anger by using past experiences or unpleasant images. This causes electricity to surge through the brain and begins the adrenaline rush.

To instantly cut your Ki off, try this: Close your eyes. Slow your deep breathing. Relax your mind and body. Conjure up a feeling of peace and happiness. This will stop the adrenaline rush.

Note: You can use your heart rate as a guide in determining your progress. You should notice an increase in your heart rate after activating your Ki. Likewise, you should notice a decrease in your heart rate when deactivating your Ki. Great masters of mind and body can increase and decrease their heart rate at will.

Ever notice how wide open a so-called maniac's eyes are when he or she flies into a rage? Well, emerging victorious from a violent attack on the streets might require you to become a maniac yourself.

In self-defense, there is only one rule to concern yourself with—there are no rules! If necessary, you must develop the ability to switch instantly from a rational human being into an unstoppable psychopath who is determined to incapacitate a ferocious attacker at any and all costs! The thought of inflicting pain on a human may be brutal and uncomfortable, but it could save your life.

The loser of a physical fight is the one whose adrenaline flow has been shut off. And, by now you should realize that the development of focus and concentration is critical to your success as a fighter. The truth is that effective fighting is more about controlling your mind and emotions than controlling your body.

Great truths are long-lasting. Very few concepts are truly original. Some people just dig a little deeper into the cause and effect, which allows them to see something previously undiscovered. Always remember: Everything on earth is *discovered* as new. Nothing is ever *invented* as new. It was always there in its raw form. Someone has simply discovered its presence and made use of it, by discovering its capabilities and applications. Use this truth as motivation for self-development.

The following drills will increase your ability to recognize and track fast movements. You will also learn to concentrate for increasingly longer periods of time. It is this stamina of the mind that really determines your level of physical stamina.

Few people push their bodies to the limit because their minds give out first. In truth, your mind can be trained to concentrate for such long periods of time that your body will collapse from exhaustion. Again, it is a matter of focus and concentration.

Record Read

For this drill you will need a record player. They are rarely used these days, but you can ask friends or relatives if they have one. If not, you can probably locate one online or at a pawnshop. Club DJs are a good source to find out where you can purchase a turntable or record player because many of them still use 12-inch LPs. You can also search online. It may take a while, but it's worth it to take advantage of this excellent drill.

Practice reading the label of a record while it is spinning on the turntable. For older record players, first try the drill at 33 revolutions per minute. Later you can progress to 45 r.p.m. and then 78 r.p.m. Newer, high-quality turntables will have a lever that you can use to adjust the speed.

Try to read the song titles and any information on the label. Vary the records to avoid knowing what the label reads beforehand. You will only hamper your progress if you do not drill realistically. Practicing this a few minutes at a time will greatly increase your ability to track fast-moving objects such as punches, kicks, baseballs, tennis balls, hockey pucks, etc.

Number Flash

Take a large piece of paper and write down 20 four-digit numbers in a vertical column. Now take a card or another piece of paper large enough to cover about five numbers at a time. Cover the first few numbers. Quickly slide the card down far enough to see the first number only. Leave the card down just long enough to get a glimpse of that first number, then quickly slide the card back up to cover the number again.

You should now immediately call out the number you saw. Check to see if you were right by sliding the card down again, revealing the first number. The object is to quickly see and distinguish the number. After the first number, you can continue down the column, trying to snatch, glance, and remember each individual number before calling it out.

If you find that you are consistently off, try the drill using three-digit numbers. You can also remove the card more slowly, giving you more time to recognize the number. Do whatever it takes to give your eyes the proper challenge. Do not make it too easy.

Occasionally, you should write down new numbers to make certain you are not guessing based on memory. Later, as your recognition skills improve, you can graduate to five-, six-, and even seven-digit numbers. This will keep your eyes consistently challenged and improving.

Point Focus

For this drill you will need a sheet of paper and a pencil, pen, or marker. Mark the paper with many dots that are about one-half inch apart. Tape the paper to a wall at face level. Stand about six feet from the paper and begin to shadow fight while keeping your eyes focused on a predetermined dot of your choice.

The object is to bob, weave, punch, kick, shuffle, etc., without losing eye contact with the dot you have chosen to focus on. Move slowly at first and speed up as your focus skills improve. You can move farther away from the paper or increase the number of dots on the paper to increase the difficulty of this drill.

The Sixth Sense

Is there really a sixth sense within all of us? I believe there is, but not in the way that most people perceive its existence. I feel that the state we are in when the so-called sixth sense is functioning is simply the state of heightened subconscious functioning.

When fighting with the subconscious functioning unobstructed, you are capable of perceiving events and actions before they actually happen. It is as if you have tapped into some sort of extra-sensory perception.

E.S.P. should more appropriately be labeled D.S.P., because it is really *developed* sensory perception—not *extra*-sensory perception. Everyone possesses this amazing sense to some degree. The difference is that some have nurtured its power and some have not. Those who have not made conscious use of the sixth sense may have been unaware or skeptical of its existence.

For the speed student, the sixth sense is used to develop "anticipation skill." This is the ability to anticipate something happening before actual movement occurs. It is really a mental phenomenon. You are connecting your mind with the opponent's mind, so that you can read his or her innermost thoughts before they are initiated.

The following drills were developed for the purpose of improving your anticipation skills.

TV Response

In this drill you may use punches, kicks, or footwork for your responses. Full power should not be used because you will only be striking air. (Always hit a target when practicing power movements.)

A television will be needed for this drill. Stand about eight feet from the television. Turn on a program that has a lot of action, such as a fast-paced cartoon or action movie.

Turn the volume all the way down. You only want to *see* the show—not hear it. You should notice the picture changing constantly from one camera shot to another. Every time the picture changes, punch or kick as fast as you can in response to the change. Immediately resume your starting position and respond to the next change.

You can use something as simple as a jab or front kick.

React every time the camera shot changes. Do not think about it, or try to anticipate it—just react! Your goal is to reduce the lag time between the camera change and your punch or kick.

Eventually you will notice that it seems as though you are punching at the same time the camera shot is changing. This skill is vital to success in competition and self-defense.

Keep your mind clear and try to stick with every change of the scene. You should keep your body relaxed and your movements as smooth as possible. Practice this drill for as long as you can maintain the constant reaction to the scene changes. Stop and rest if you begin to get sloppy or tired. Practicing sloppy movements will only retard your progress as it pertains to speed and reflex development.

Traffic Light

While driving or riding in a vehicle, you can work on your anticipation skills by reacting when the traffic light changes from red to green. You can respond with a light "ugh" when the light changes. Do not try to anticipate the green light. Just react. Race car drivers use this drill to develop anticipation skill.

Caution: Do not react by slamming the gas pedal to the floor. Use an appropriate and safe response to avoid injuring anyone.

Video Games

Many athletes use video games to enhance their reaction speed. There are many sophisticated video games on the market today. Do some research by going online and/or visiting your local video game retailer. After testing a few games, choose the ones that are enjoyable and challenging to your reflexes.

Pet Snatch

You can enhance your anticipation skills with the help of a pet. Simply hold a rag slightly above a playful dog or cat. When your pet tries to jump for the rag, jerk it away. As you do, simultaneously respond with a silent "ugh." (Definitely do not try this with an unfamiliar animal, no matter how fast you become!)

In the initial stages, you can hold the rag high. As your reaction time improves, you can lower the rag closer to your pet for a greater challenge.

Focus Glove Snatch

For this drill, you can use a focus glove or your bare hand. Be particularly careful if using your bare hands. Do not strike the hand with full power. Personally, I feel this drill is more beneficial when a focus pad is used.

Place a glove on one of your hands. As your partner attempts to strike the pad, jerk it away.

Tell your partner to go for speed rather than power. He or she should not try to fake you out in order to hit the pad. That is not the purpose of this drill. Your partner should just stand calmly, and try to beat you to the punch by hitting the pad before you can move it. After each attempt, both of you should resume starting positions.

If your partner keeps hitting the pad, take a step back. As your response time improves, you can move the pad closer.

Another form of this drill is to have your partner try to close the gap on you, before you can evade the attack. This drill depends primarily on footwork, but it also depends on anticipation skill. There is no punching or kicking involved. Simply have your opponent lunge forward as quickly as possible. You should anticipate the movement and evade it before your partner moves. Resume starting positions and repeat. No fakes or feinting.

As you improve, you can move closer to your partner. You will find that this drill enhances agility as well as anticipation skill.

Diligent practice of these drills will enable you to beat your adversaries to the punch, even when they throw their punches first! I guarantee you will be surprised how these simple drills can shorten your response time.

The Focus Point

When fighting, you need a focus point. This aids in helping your Ki function at its maximum level. The best focus point is the opponent's eyes if you want to perceive an attack as quickly as possible. The next best focus point is the torso area, because it shows you what direction the opponent's attack is coming from. Use the eyes as a focus point for long-distance fighting and the torso during close fighting and grappling.

At a distance, you should concentrate intensely on your opponent's eyes, as if you are trying to see right through them and read his or her mind. You will be surprised to find yourself doing just that!

The stronger your concentration, the easier it will be for you to read an opponent's mind. You can test this theory yourself. First, try the previous anticipation drills while focusing on the arms, legs, or any part of your opponent other than the eyes. You will see how slow your reactions can be. Now, try the same drills while focusing intensely on your opponent's eyes. You should also turn on your Ki. You will now be able to anticipate your opponent's moves more easily.

Note: If you are facing multiple attackers, you must make use of your peripheral vision. However, you should still focus on the eyes of the one opponent you are facing at each moment.

Chapter 3

Tactile Reflexes

Tactile reflexes involve the ability to quickly react to the stimulus of touch. It is the attribute referred to as "sensitivity" in martial arts.

Ninety-five percent of all streetfights will end up in the close distance and/or grappling range. In this range, it is not likely that you will "see" the attack coming. With tactile reflexes, you will not need to see where your hands are in relation to your adversary—because you will "feel" your position in relation to your opponent.

With practice, you will learn to instantly feel what the opponent is attempting to do by quickly reading the direction of his body force. Using this awareness, you can take the opponent's energy and do one of three things:

1. Dissolve the energy (by evading or and slipping).

2. Redirect the energy (by blocking or parrying).

3. Crash the energy (by stop-hitting or countering).

To make maximum use of your tactile reflexes, it is imperative that you stay relaxed when you come into contact with the opponent. It is through relaxation that you will find speed and explosiveness in your actions.

Tactile reflexes are usually highly developed in people who study such arts as Judo, Jujitsu, Wing Chun, Kali, Wrestling, and Aikido. To maximize your tactile reflexes: you should train in martial arts that emphasize close-range fighting.

Sensitivity Drills

There are many drills that you can use to develop your tactile reflexes. However, be careful not to get caught up in the drill itself. The drills are only a means to an end. Your purpose is to develop superior tactile reflexes that will enable you to easily dominate an opponent in the closer fighting ranges.

It is difficult to learn sensitivity from a book or a video. You will do best to find a partner who is familiar with the drills of martial arts that specialize in the in-fighting, close-quarter, trapping, and grappling ranges. The drills you choose are important, but the effort you put into each drill is just as important.

Secret: To get better results from any sensitivity drill, try it blindfolded. This forces you to heighten your sense of touch, which will lead to rapid improvement in your tactile reflexes.

The following are basic drills for developing tactile sensitivity.

Single Hand Sensitivity Drill

Take your fighting position. Have your training partner do the same. Now, you should both extend your lead fighting hands until they are touching at the wrist (like two swords that are crossed). Place your rear hand behind your back.

Now, both of you should close your eyes. Relax. Try to feel each other's energy for a while. The primary goal is to stay in contact with your partner's hand.

Have your partner try to disengage (leave) your hand and strike your torso. If you are relaxed and aware of your partner's energy, you should not be struck. You should successfully "stick" to your partner's hand and prevent him or her from striking you. Resume starting positions and begin again. Remember to keep your eyes closed.

As your tactile reflexes improve, you can move closer and closer to the opponent with this drill.

Double Hand Sensitivity Drill

Take a fighting position. Engage both of your partners' hands with both of your hands. Relax. Now try to quickly, but lightly, strike your partner by leaving or tying up his or her hands. Your partner should attempt to do the same. Remember to not strain. Relaxation is the key to speed.

Blind Grappling

Start off with both you and your partner blindfolded. Now engage each other from a wrestling position until you can both feel each other's arms and legs.

Try to take your partner down by feeling his or her energy and seizing the perfect moment when your partner is pushing or pulling in the wrong direction. This requires an acute awareness.

In competition or self-defense, you have only a split second to feel the energy as your partner gets closer. At long range, you should be relaxed and patient while waiting to attack. But as the gap closes, you should become instantaneously more focused, explosive, and relentless in your attack.

Secret: The key to maximizing an attribute rapidly is to isolate the attribute, and force it to adapt to consistently increasing demands. After doing these drills with your eyes closed, you will notice that your awareness is heightened when reverting back to doing drills with your eyes open.

Chapter 4

Auditory Reflexes

Auditory reflexes concern your ability to react quickly to what you hear. This skill is useful in situations where you have to defend yourself in the dark. In this situation, it is more likely that you will hear the attack before you see it. Auditory reflexes will also help you when defending against multiple attackers.

Having highly developed auditory reflexes is the closest thing to having eyes in the back of your head.

Fully developing all of your senses is a key goal of speed training. When your senses are functioning at their peak, you will find yourself reacting first and then thinking—as opposed to thinking first and then reacting.

Experiments indicate that auditory cues, when occurring close to the athlete, are responded to more quickly than visual cues. People without sight, through daily living, are forced to develop their listening skills to advanced levels. For those of us with the gift of sight, we must artificially create the circumstances that will force us to cultivate our critical listening skills for competition and self-defense purposes.

Auditory Reflex Drills

Basic Sound Trigger

You will need a partner for this drill. Start by assuming a ready position. Close your eyes. Have your partner quickly shout out any word. When you detect a shout is about to happen, react as fast as you can, with a punch or a kick. After assuming a ready position again, you should say "ready," to let your partner know that you are ready for the next shout. Have your partner pause as long as desired before quickly shouting a word again.

This drill will develop the basic neurological responses for auditory reflex development.

Eventually, you will be reacting before your partner can finish saying the word.

Intermediate Sound Trigger

This drill is like the basic drill, except you and your partner should choose one word that you will react to. Now, what your partner must do is quickly shout out the chosen word—but only periodically. Other words should be shouted out, between the chosen word, in an attempt to make you respond.

You should react only to the chosen word. Again, make certain that your partner waits until you say, "ready" before word shouting begins. This drill will develop your ability to control your auditory reflexes.

Advanced Sound Trigger

The only difference between this drill and the intermediate drill is that your partner should lower the volume. This will force you to concentrate even harder in order to hear the chosen word. Have your training partner lower the volume as you improve.

One way to make these drills more challenging is to abandon the ready stance and inject some reality. Sit down and read a paper or book. Act as if you are out at the movies or a restaurant. Have your partner shout quickly. React by initiating your attack as fast as you can from various positions.

Imagine that you are being attacked as you enter your car or as you are walking down the street talking to a friend. You must make full use of your best teacher, your imagination. Also, you must continue to systematically increase the difficulty of all drills in order to push your speed to the maximum.

The whole idea is to learn to instantly explode into action from any position in response to an auditory cue that demands immediate reaction.

Solo Sound Trigger

You can also practice this drill on your own if you have access to a voice recorder. Simply record yourself shouting a word over and over. Make certain you pause long enough between shouts to give yourself time to get ready again. Also, it is very important to vary the rhythm between shouts so that you can't anticipate them.

You can practice this drill with your eyes closed to help you stay focused on the sound. You can also keep your eyes open and use your imagination for situational training. It's up to you. Be creative in your approach to training and self-improvement. Let results be the deciding factor as to whether something is working.

Learning to Listen

You can improve your auditory reflexes by simply learning to listen more closely to what goes on around you in your daily life. Listen to a conversation between people across the room. Close your eyes and try to distinguish what is being said.

Take a walk outside and take note of sounds you can hear. Listen for cars humming, birds singing, wind blowing, kids playing, dogs barking, etc. Listen to the radio at low volume levels. Try to detect what is being said or sung. You are training your ears to become more acute. At this time, medical science can't improve your actual hearing capacity—but you can improve your ability to be more aware of what you can already hear.

The following are steps you can take to prevent hearing loss:

- Be aware of and avoid harmful noise.
- Use hearing protection when exposed to harmful noise levels.
- Minimize your total daily exposure to harmful noise levels.
- Control the volume when you can.
- Never stick objects in your ear.
- Always blow your nose gently.
- Ask your doctor if any of the medications you may be taking have hearing-related side effects.

Chapter 5

Adaptation Speed

This chapter will improve the quickness and accuracy of your mind. You will develop the ability to instantaneously select the most effective movements to use at any point during a confrontation. You will learn to do this without thought. Your reflexes will carry out the movement selection process automatically.

Obviously, adaptation speed is a crucial link in the Speed Loop™. Without adaptation speed, you could perceive an attack or opening, but you would react improperly. Even with great movement speed, you must have adaptation speed to be effective. You cannot initiate a movement until you (consciously or unconsciously) think about it first! Your goal is to transfer all of your simple responses and reactions from conscious to unconscious functioning. The achievement of this one goal will double your speed.

Stick Training

Training with escrima sticks, as is taught in conjunction with the Filipino martial arts, is one of the best ways to increase your adaptation speed. Under the guidance of a competent instructor, you can elevate your speed and reflexes to a phenomenal level in a relatively short period of time. If an instructor is not readily available, I suggest you purchase DVDs or videos, attend seminars on the Filipino martial arts, and practice the basics with a partner.

You do not need to know every detail of the art. Just gather enough to help you gain a better understanding of the angles and the concept of "flowing." As you will see, these arts (like all effective combat systems) are based primarily on speed of flow, economy of motion, and spiritual involvement. All are attributes of the superior fighter.

Stick training (Filipino style) will definitely push your speed and reflexes to new heights. Using a stick, you can attack an opponent from multiple angles in a split second. The stick is so fast because all you need to do is flick your wrist to instantly change the angle of attack. No one can punch or kick as fast as they can flip the end of a stick at a target.

Wielded by a trained specialist, the stick has been consistently clocked at speeds well over 150 m.p.h. Compare this to the relatively slow 100 m.p.h. of the so-called fastballs thrown in major league baseball!

This leads me to the next reason why you, as a speed student, should look into the Filipino martial arts. They teach angles as opposed to techniques.

All techniques, regardless of their stylized characteristics, will travel along the path of one of the 12 angles of attack identified in the Filipino martial arts. Accordingly, all openings presented to you will be along these same 12 angles. By dealing with common angles, and not individual techniques, you will dramatically reduce your reaction choices. Fewer choices to sort through in response to an attack or opening will lead to quicker responses.

After training with the sticks and reverting back to empty hands, you will notice that your opponent's empty hand actions will seem to move in slow motion. Because of your improved reflexes, they *will* be slower. This sensation can be compared to the experience of driving at 100 m.p.h. and then slowing down to 65 m.p.h. Even though 65 m.p.h. is not that slow, it feels slow because you've been functioning in a faster realm. It is the same with fluid stick training. You should use this slow motion sensation as a gauge of progress. The slower things seem to be, the faster you are becoming.

The best preparation for actual fighting is full-contact sparring (with adequate protective gear). With the gear and escrima sticks, you and your partner will easily cut your reaction times in half. In the short time needed to learn the basics of these arts, you will see noticeable improvement in most of your fighting attributes.

I guarantee you will learn to move very fast when a sizeable piece of wood is coming at you at more than 150 m.p.h.! Needless to say, you will give your all to avoid it, and eliminate its operator as quickly and efficiently as possible. No time will be wasted, and I am certain that you will be truly functioning at 100% of your innate ability.

An important aspect of the Filipino arts is the "flow." To ensure maximum development of your flow, it is imperative that you start off slowly and speed up as your coordination improves with the stick. Focus on maintaining proper form and using economy of motion.

The validity of stick training for the speed student is evident when observed closely. As you have learned, to develop an attribute quickly, you must consistently push the attribute slightly beyond its current capabilities. This tears the attribute down and is called Phase One of the development. Phase One is active development.

Between these periods of active development, you should get proper rest. Resting is Phase Two of the attribute's development. During this phase, the attribute (speed, power, strength, or stamina) actually improves and prepares itself to accept an increased workload. In other words, it is rebuilding itself to its original level and beyond. Phase Two is a passive form of development, but it is crucial and often ignored by most novices.

In weight training, the recognition and effective application of the work period (Phase One) and rest period (Phase Two) is called "cycling." It is a proven method for accelerating physical development. Use this concept in your speed training.

When training, you must concentrate on using economy of motion in your actions. Be direct and simple. The purpose is not to practice proper form for the sake of looking good, at least not for the speed student. All fights are bound to get sloppy. The objective in training is to practice good form for the sake of economy of motion, which directly increases speed.

Focus Gloves

Focus gloves are valuable tools that will help you develop mental speed. I recommend purchasing a training DVD or video that instructs you on the proper use of the focus gloves.

You will need a partner to get the most out of focus glove training. The better your partner is at manipulating focus gloves, the better you will get at hitting them. The idea is to force your mind to instantly strike the pad from any angle that your partner holds it at. Most people make the mistake of rigidly practicing with the pads. They hold them as if they were a heavy bag. The pads are best used for "active movement" training.

The key is to adapt to the pads—not to make them adapt to you! Initially, focus glove training will prove to be the source of much frustration. But, I promise you that within weeks you will notice a significant improvement in your mental speed. Do not cheat yourself! You must be patient and start off slowly and in good form. You can speed up as your adaptation speed improves. Ask your partner to take note of any bad habits you have, such as not pulling your punches back, or dropping your hands. You want to correct as many bad habits in training as you can because you won't have that opportunity in a real fight.

The following is one of my favorite focus glove drills for developing mental quickness and adaptation speed.

Number Call

For this drill, have your partner hold the focus gloves still. Pick a number for each type of punch. A jab could be number one, a cross could be two, a hook could be three, an uppercut could be four. Now have your partner call out a number at random. You must respond by executing the strike designated for that particular number as fast as you possibly can. Your partner should vary the tone of voice and the rhythm at which the numbers are called in order to make it as challenging as possible for you without making it too difficult.

This drill will virtually drive you crazy at first, but progress will come fast. You are in the process of tuning up your mind. If you find that four numbers are too many to start with, try it with three or two. As your adaptation speed improves, add more numbers. Use kicks, punches, elbows, knees, head butts, or whatever else you come up with by designating a number for each. Be creative and always strive to make your training intense, but enjoyable.

Mixed Sparring

Mixed sparring is a great way to increase your adaptation speed quickly. Like stick fighting, mixed sparring forces you to improve rapidly because it taps into your basic instincts. You will see results twice as fast by practicing with someone who is faster than you. Do not fall into the ego trap of sparring with people who are nowhere near your equal. They, not you, will benefit from this!

In mixed sparring, one person is allowed to use only the lead hand, and the opponent is allowed to use all limbs. The person using all limbs only has to focus on the lead hand as a threat, but the one-handed fighter has to be aware of an infinite number of techniques. Consequently, awareness is heightened and adaptation speed improves. You can practice this drill with either fast and light contact or full contact (and proper protective gear).

I have repeatedly stressed the point of training with someone who is faster than you, but if you can't find anyone, mixed sparring with a slower training partner is an acceptable alternative. After practicing mixed sparring for a while, you will become so mentally sharp that you will be able to defeat some opponents with just your lead hand, although I would not advise you to try this in competition or self-defense.

Mental Shadowfighting

Your imagination can be a very effective teacher. But, some people are not receptive to new ideas and teachings. If you want to tap the power of imagination, you will have to keep an open mind.

The imagination must be exercised like any other muscle. Being pressured to learn something that you really want to learn anyway is very effective. It might surprise you to find out how quickly you could learn a new language if you happened to find yourself alone and lost in another part of the world. The experience and assimilation would be unlike any language course you could find.

So you see, the imagination is something that you must be motivated to use. Once you are sufficiently motivated, learning becomes faster and easier.

Although you can develop speed in the shortest possible time by training with someone who is faster, the next best choice is an imaginary partner who is faster.

Predator Drill

Envision yourself being attacked by one or more muggers. As they close in, you explode into action and defeat them handily. Concentrate on seeing yourself adapting to their every move with ease and explosiveness. I like to call it "fighting the Predator."

For some, these mental pictures will be difficult to produce, but you must keep running them in your mind, until you can vividly see yourself moving as fast as you would like to.

It is very important that you react to the first technique that pops into your head to defeat the opponent's attack. Do not slow the pictures down either, unless you are working on a specific move or technique. Do not think about it, just react!

Your mind will be clicking from one technique to another at an astonishing rate. Try to adapt to every attack that you envision, as best as you can, until you have finally emerged victorious over the "Predator."

Work yourself up into a genuine fighting frame of mind. Try to react every time the picture changes. Continue this drill for as long as you can maintain the constant reaction to the change of attacks popping in your mind. If you begin to get tired or sloppy, stop and rest. Remember, quality of training is more important than quantity when it comes to developing speed.

Did you know you can accomplish nearly anything you can imagine? If you can't, it is most often because you really can't see it vividly. To see it clearly you must be highly motivated. Every physical action that we carry out is simply a duplication of the pictures that occupy our minds at the moment. The faster you can picture yourself moving, the faster you will move. I know this concept sounds a little far-fetched, but it's absolutely true. It has been tested and confirmed countless times. You can experiment with it yourself.

How fast do you want to be? You should clearly see yourself moving as fast as you would like to move. Do not visualize someone else. You must see yourself moving at lightning speed. You will probably find that this mental picture of your blazing speed will be difficult to see clearly if you do not truly believe that you are that fast. This is where the problem lies. If you cannot see it, how do you expect to duplicate it?

Mental speed training is an important part of the Speed Loop™. Keep visualizing yourself moving faster and faster. If you do, the picture will get clearer, and as a consequence, you will actually become faster.

Environmental Training

Environmental Training will take your adaptation speed to new levels of proficiency by increasing the balance of your "technique bank." Your technique bank is simply the place in your brain where all of the techniques you have ever seen, done, or visualized are stored. It is similar to a digital camera or iPod™ storing pictures or music. Environmental training will help you develop the ability to automatically "dial up" the right techniques at the right time.

Most fighters are very proficient defending against a particular style of fighter, in a particular type of setting. However, *a superior fighter is one who can successfully adapt to any style of fighting in any kind of setting.* That is the essence of applied adaptation speed!

Can you defend yourself against a grappler as quickly as against a boxer? Against a streetfighter as quickly as against a Thai Boxer? Against a knife as quickly as against a stick?

To maximize speed for competition and self-defense, I do not recommend studying only one style of fighting for a prolonged period. It is likely that using the training methods of one style will lead to small improvements in speed. Superior fighters know that training in mixed martial arts is the best way to maximize speed.

It is vitally important to understand that the movement speed used in a controlled environment for the purpose of inducing "oohs" and "ahhs" from spectators, is a lot different than the applied speed needed for success in competition and self-defense.

During environmental training, your goal is to consciously put yourself in unfamiliar situations and to respond as quickly as possible.

You can start by sparring against different styles of fighting. Do not get into the bad habit of working with only one training partner. After a short period of time, you will both know each other's strengths and weaknesses, and you will not be adapting anymore. You will be doing more anticipating—a trap that won't be so easy to fall into when training against an unfamiliar opponent.

The next phase of environmental training is to break away from the conventional sparring mode. This means no face-offs, no uniforms, no stylistic rules, and no time limits. First, you should make a list of 10-15 combat scenarios. For instance: fighting from a bar stool, fighting from a toilet, fighting from a bed as you wake up, fighting a raging and cursing lunatic who just escaped from a mental hospital, fighting from your car, fighting with a broken leg or arm. Put your imagination to work; potential situations are endless.

From there, work with different training partners to play out the fighting scenarios. Again, the idea is to get familiar with as many situations as possible, to better balance your technique bank. This type of environmental training will put you on the fast track to developing advanced speed.

Secret: The ultimate in applied advanced speed is the ability to adapt quickly and effectively to any fighting situation, at any time, at any place, against any adversary. For all of you impressed by the crisp snapping sound of your uniform when practicing solo: Stop fooling yourself and get real! Challenge yourself in a realistic way today if you want victories tomorrow!

Chapter 6

Initiation Speed

This chapter will improve your quickness and explosiveness. You will learn all about non-telegraphing and economy of motion.

Initiation speed must precede movement speed if your attack is to be successful. It's not how fast you move, but how soon you get there that counts! Your attack may be very fast in flight, but a slow takeoff will severely reduce your chances of effectively landing that attack on target.

The application of the drills and concepts in this section will ensure the connection of your attack to the opponent before a countermove can be attempted. Once you reach this point, you will know (as all advanced speed students do) that the hand is quicker than the eye.

Relaxation

The essential prerequisite for initiation speed is the ability to relax at will, even in the midst of a competitive battle.

You must learn to use your muscles economically. All too often, I see beginners pressing and straining in their actions only to find themselves getting even slower. They do this because they lack initiation speed and knowledge of critical relaxation principles.

Relaxation begins with the development of neuromuscular awareness skill, which can be broken down as follows:

1. Acquire the feeling of relaxation as compared to tension.
2. Practice in solitude until this feeling of relaxation can be reproduced at will.
3. Practice reproducing this feeling in controlled training situations (during training drills).
4. Finally, practice reproducing this feeling of instinctive relaxation in uncontrolled

fighting situations (during realistic sparring and environmental training).

The ability to feel contraction and relaxation, to know what a muscle is doing is called *kinesthetic perception*. It is developed by consciously placing your body parts in different positions and getting the "feel" of each one. This feeling of balance or imbalance, grace or awkwardness, serves as a constant guide to your body as it moves.

Your kinesthetic perception should be developed to such a high degree that the body feels uncomfortable unless it performs each motion with minimum effort to produce maximum results.

Relaxation is a physical state, but it is controlled by the mental state. Relaxation in competition and self-defense depends on the cultivation of mental focus and emotional poise in the midst of chaos. The kind of relaxation you are concerned with is that of the body, not the mind. In combat, your mind should be intensely focused, while your body should be relaxed, supple, and ready to explode in an instant.

Meditation

Meditation is indispensable to the superior fighter's success, though some will not admit it— or worse, do not realize it. There are many schools of thought on the science of meditation, but the end result is always the same: the simultaneous achievement of a relaxed body and a focused mind.

Meditation is a simple exercise. First, you should find a comfortable position. This can be lying down, sitting, or standing. Close your eyes. Now, tense your whole body, from the top of your head to the bottom of your feet, as hard as you can. Hold like this for about 5-10 seconds, then relax.

Next, take three deep breaths. Be sure to breathe slowly and naturally. Inhale deeply and exhale slowly, while pursing your lips. During the first exhalation, softly say, "Legs relax," and think and feel your legs relaxing. During the second exhalation, softly say, "Arms relax," and think and feel your arms relaxing. During the third exhalation, softly say, "Body relax," and think and feel your entire body relaxing.

If any part of you remains tense, go back and relax it by softly telling that part of your body to relax. Concentrate on keeping your breathing slow, deep, and rhythmic until you feel totally relaxed from head to toe.

At this point, you should begin to program yourself using self-hypnosis. You can do this by repeating the following suggestion at least ten times: "My total fighting speed continues to improve every day."

If you wanted to focus on improving one particular link of the speed chain, you could build your statement around that.

For instance: "My initiation speed continues to improve every day."

The statement I prepared for you is for basic fighting speed development. It can be altered as necessary to suit your needs. Athletes from all major sports have successfully used self-hypnosis to improve their speed and enhance their skills.

> **Secret:** While doing self-hypnosis, you should visualize yourself as you want to be. Concentrate intensely on seeing yourself possessing advanced speed. The scenes should look so realistic that it is like you are watching yourself in a movie.

Practice meditating once or twice a day. After you become proficient at relaxation, you will not need to practice as often. In the beginning stages, you can meditate while lying down. Once you become proficient at relaxing your body, you can meditate anywhere, at any time.

The best times to practice your self-hypnosis are just before falling asleep and immediately upon arising in the morning. At these times, you are in a natural state of hypnosis, and the suggestions will sink in more easily. The goal is to effectively input the suggestions into your subconscious. Once there, the suggestions will start to materialize through the awesome power of believing.

Be certain that your suggestions are clearly spoken. Also, make certain you put as much "feeling" into the suggestions as possible. You must talk like you really believe every word! This belief will cause the suggestions to take on the power of imperial commands. But, if you simply mouth the words half-heartedly, I guarantee you will be disappointed with the results. Remember, it's often not *what* you say, but *how* you say it that matters.

Self-hypnosis will do wonders for your physical skills. The change will not take place overnight, but there will be a noticeable change in as little time as ten days. Initially, you may not notice improvements, but your training partners will. They will feel the noticeable change in your speed and skill when they spar against you. They will observe that you seem more confident and relaxed, but they will not know why unless you tell them about your meditation exercises.

Non-Telegraphed Movement

In order to successfully connect on your opponent, you need more than blinding movement speed. You also need to develop non-telegraphed movements. The first step to non-telegraphed movement development is relaxation, which you have learned about. Now it's time to develop your ability to disguise your intentions, so that your opponent will feel the sting of your punch before seeing it. You must develop the ability to attack without warning in order to accomplish this.

It is much easier to explode into action if you are already moving slightly. It is harder, and more easily detected, if you are starting from a still position. In sparring and shadowfighting, learn to keep moving. You can keep your hands and head moving smoothly like a boxer. Not only does this disguise your intentions, it makes you a more difficult target to hit. Don't be a sitting duck by adopting a stiff and inflexible stance once the fighting has begun.

The Poker Face

The poker face is the face of no expression.

It has been said that the "eyes are the windows to the soul." A fighter has to think, consciously or unconsciously, about an action before he or she can execute it. Whatever you think is revealed in your eyes. Some people reveal much; some learn to reveal very little.

The eyes are the best focus point because they usually reveal the most about a person's intentions. As an advanced speed student, you want to know about those harmful intentions as early as possible before they are initiated.

On the flip side, it would behoove you to learn how to effectively disguise your own intentions with your eyes, so that your opponent can't detect and react to your attack in sufficient time. A lot of your offensive success in fighting will depend on your ability to deceive the opponent with your eyes.

You can practice putting on your poker face in front of a mirror to start. Later, you can practice it in your drills and in sparring. Relax and show your opponent no fear. He or she will be intimidated by you. Just gaze calmly, yet insanely, into his or her eyes as if you are a machine programmed to kill. Focus your eyes directly on your opponent's eyes, but do not let the eyes deceive you. Seek control of your opponent's psyche. Use your highly developed poker face to exhibit convincing confidence and to instill fear and caution in your opponent.

It takes practice to develop a truly strong and deceptive poker face. Concentration is absolutely essential! Once you have developed a good poker face, your opponents will find it very difficult to figure you out and gauge your attack (which is exactly what you want). When humans cannot figure something out, we have a tendency to become uncomfortable and fearful. We start to think really hard about whatever it is that's mystifying us. It is at that point, when we start thinking too hard, that we lose our ability to adapt and go with the flow.

That is when we are most vulnerable. That is exactly where you want your opponent. That is the best time to attack!

By developing a good poker face, you will diminish the opponent's ability to anticipate the proper time to attack you. You will also take away his or her ability to effectively anticipate your attacks. Your opponent will be forced to rely strictly on movement speed when he or she can't read you. If this is the case, I guarantee you will hit your opponent almost every time!

Initiation Drills

A good way to develop your initiation speed is by practicing shadowfighting in front of a mirror. Pay close attention to your facial expressions and the degree of tension in your muscles. Most people lose their poker face when they launch an attack. They twitch an eye, grit their teeth, or make a slight gesture, which is all your opponent needs to react. Be patient. It will take some time to develop the ability to maintain an ultra-cool poker face while on the move.

Another good way to develop initiation speed is by practicing the focus glove snatch drill from chapter two of this guide. The person holding the glove will be developing their visual reflexes and ability to read intentions. The person trying to strike the glove can work on quickness and the ability to disguise intentions.

You and your training partner should both strive to get benefits from every drill practiced together. You will find that all good drills benefit certain attributes for both partners. The key is to identify those attributes and concentrate on improving them during the drills.

Explosiveness

Explosiveness is the ability to relay destructiveness in a sudden manner. It is a combination of speed and power. This is the last step in the development of your initiation speed. The following are the drills that will enhance your explosiveness.

The Book Drop

At first, try this drill while standing. Hold any book about six inches in front of your face. Drop the book by opening your fingers and thumb. Don't throw it, just let it fall naturally.

When you let go, punch as quickly as possible, and then pull your punch back just as fast, so that you can grab the book before it hits the floor. It's not as easy as you may think.

You really don't need great movement speed for this drill. You do need initiation speed and economical explosiveness. Relaxation is essential. If you're tense, you will have a much harder time catching the book as it falls.

Be certain to drop the book *before* you punch. Do not punch while holding the book so that it flips or flies across the room before descending. Also, your punch should be fully extended before you attempt to retrieve the book as it falls.

You really have to relax when extending and retracting your hand to avoid smacking the book to the floor. It requires relaxed concentration to drop, punch and grasp in a split-second.

If you have difficulty doing this drill, try extending the book farther from your face before dropping it. This way, your punch will not have to cover as much distance, and you should be able to get back quickly enough to clutch the book before it falls.

If the original drill becomes too easy, you can increase the difficulty by reducing the distance the book has to fall. Try the drill while sitting or kneeling. You will have to move very fast to drop the book, punch fully, and clutch the book before it can fall to the floor.

You could also stand directly in front of a table that you can hold the book over. This will reduce the distance the book has to fall, and make it harder for you to clutch it before it hits the table.

Inch Training

Inch training is one of the best ways to develop your explosiveness. Start by having your partner hold, at chest level, two focus gloves or an air shield for you to strike. Put your fist to the target. Pull your fist approximately six inches from the target. Now—explode! Strike through the target as fast and as deep as you can without dissolving your strike into a push. Make the strike a swift and penetrating snap. You only want to go a couple of inches into the target.

If you explode correctly, your partner should be able to feel the penetrating force of your punch. Your partner should brace for the anticipated strike.

You should first relax, put on your poker face, and then picture yourself exploding through the target in your mind before your partner can tense up. Be certain to practice exploding with all of your tools. Use punches, kicks, elbows, knees, forearms, and head butts.

Heavy Bag

Another great tool for explosiveness is the heavy bag. Contrary to popular belief, the heavy bag will not slow you down. Those who claim that the heavy bag does slow you down simply do not know how to use this invaluable tool correctly.

To be fast, you must think fast and move fast. Working with the heavy bag is no exception to this rule.

Sure, if you hit the heavy bag with only "haymakers" or power punches, you will not get any faster. You will not get any slower either. You might get the feeling that you are slower after a heavy bag session. This is because the heavy bag is capable of working nearly every muscle in your body. Unlike punching in the air, hitting the heavy bag involves more muscular exertion, which causes fatigue to set in quicker. Naturally, a more fatigued muscle is a slower one. But, working with the heavy bag will give you the ability to move faster for a longer period of time.

When utilized correctly, the heavy bag will improve your stamina, power, explosiveness, distance, timing, *and speed*. It's actually the next best thing to a training partner.

The key to the heavy bag (and any other training tool) is to concentrate on the attribute you want to develop. To develop speed and explosiveness, you must hit the bag with quick, sharp, and explosive combinations. Do not telegraph your strikes or try to put too much power into them. Relax and throw your shots from all angles. Be sure to snap your punches and kicks as opposed to merely pushing them. Novice students of the heavy bag often ignore this very important point.

Treat the bag as alive and active! Move with it. Dodge it. Circle it. Push it off of you. Lean on it. Smack it. If you use your imagination (like all superior fighters), you will find yourself feeling like you're in a real fight with the heavy bag. Your goal is to make that bag give you some benefits.

Do not settle for less than that from any training tool!

After working on explosiveness for a couple of weeks, you will notice that you no longer have to draw your punches and kicks back before releasing them in order to relay destructiveness. You will come to realize that pulling a punch back before releasing it actually reduces its power. The extra distance causes you to use scattered energy as opposed to the much more powerful focused energy, which is created out of condensed space and relaxation. Focused energy is the secret of all great knockout artists, whether they applied it consciously or unconsciously.

An example of focused energy at work in everyday life would be the following: Let's say you have one week to prepare a report for school or work, and you estimate you can finish it in four days. If you are anything like ninety-eight percent of the population, you will probably not start on it immediately. A lot of people would start working on the report one day before it is due.

If you were in this situation, you would first have to relax. Then, you would need to focus intensely on the task at hand. I bet you would probably finish the report on time, regardless of how late you had to stay awake. On the other hand, some people might dabble over the report for the whole week in order to finish it.

In actual application, focused energy not only saves time, but also improves performance. Start applying focused energy to your daily life and start reaping the many benefits it has to offer.

Wrist and Ankle Weights

With proper caution, you can quickly improve the delivery of your punches and kicks with the use of light wrist weights and ankle weights.

Warning: Practicing these drills incorrectly and without caution can result in injury. Do not practice these drills if you suffer from any type of joint pain. **You are strongly encouraged to consult a physician before practicing these drills**. When practicing these drills, be very careful not to hyperextend your punches or kicks to avoid injuring your elbows, shoulders, knees, or hips. Do not throw full-power punches or kicks because it may cause injury. Use your common sense and learn to listen to your body's signals of pain or strain. **Stop the workout and contact a medical professional immediately if you feel joint pain or unusual fatigue.**

To start, you will need a pair of one-pound wrist weights. Start with a round of shadowboxing using only punches, elbows, and any other techniques that are executed with the arms. The round can last as long as you want, but one minute of intense shadowfighting is better than three minutes of lackadaisical shadowfighting.

Next, strap on one-pound or two-pound ankle weights and proceed with a round of shadowkicking. Use various striking techniques with your feet and knees.

Finally, go through a round of shadowfighting using all of your tools while wearing the wrist weights and ankle weights.

The purpose of these drills is to develop the explosive blows that are characteristic of superior fighters.

If you keep your body relaxed, you will notice that your punches and kicks automatically snap back at the end of delivery. After training with the wrist weights and ankle weights for a while, you will notice that your punches are not only faster, but also more powerful and explosive.

Chapter 7

Movement Speed

Movement speed is the ability to quickly transition from one point to another. Your movement speed is determined by your ability to contract and relax your muscles efficiently. This is the type of speed most readily recognized by the untrained fighter or the public at large.

Most novice fighters place too much emphasis on movement speed. What they don't realize is that movement speed (without visual reflexes, mental reflexes, auditory reflexes, initiation speed, and all the other Speed Loop™ components) does not ensure success in competition or self-defense.

To impress prospective students, deceptive martial arts instructors will frequently use speed demonstrations. The uninformed are often led to believe that movement speed is the key attribute to have, because it can be easily displayed and observed. The other types of speed are not so easy to demonstrate and most often they can't be seen. Instead, the practitioner must *feel* them.

Contrary to popular belief, blinding movement speed is not absolutely necessary for success in competition or self-defense. Do not be misled by staged demonstrations or choreographed fight scenes that utilize sophisticated computer and video technology.

If you have ever witnessed a real fight, you know things do not go as smoothly as we sometimes see on the big screen. Streetfights are not rehearsed. Consequently, they are intensely awkward and slow compared to movie scenes, demonstrations, or training drills. The stress and fear of real bodily harm causes our muscles to tighten and we become somewhat anxious in our actions, even if we have trained for years. It's the natural *fight-or-flight response.*

So, why even bother to develop your movement speed? Because you will move faster in a streetfight than you will if you don't develop it. However, you should remember that you would not move as fast as you do in training, since you cannot reproduce the same level of stress caused by a real physically threatening confrontation. The best way to mimic real confrontation conditions is to engage in full-contact environmental sparring (with protective gear). This forces you to move fast while trying to manage the effects of the adrenaline rush on your mind and body.

Secret: Flexibility plays a key role in your ability to extend and retract quickly. You should adopt a progressive stretching program if you want to achieve superior movement speed.

Extension Speed

Movement speed has multiple components. To realize your full speed potential, you must break down each one of these components and work with it separately. This is the isolation principle of development.

The first component of movement speed is *extension speed*. Extension speed is your ability to quickly "lengthen" your muscles through contraction and relaxation. Throwing a jab or a front kick from your ready position is an example of extension speed.

The best way to develop extension speed is to practice drills and techniques while consciously focusing on throwing them faster each time. When training, pay close attention to the level of tension in your muscles as you move. There is an optimum state that is the perfect balance between muscle contraction and muscle relaxation. Finding this optimum state of muscle tension will maximize your movement speed when launching an attack.

Retraction Speed

Retraction Speed is your ability to quickly "shorten" your muscles through contraction and relaxation. Pulling your jab or front kick back after it has landed is an example of retraction speed.

One immediate way to increase your retraction speed is to practice recoiling or snapping your hand or foot back to its original position. Focus on pulling your hand or foot back faster than it went out. Imagine your strikes rebounding off the target after connecting.

The following drills will greatly improve your extension and retraction speed.

The Paper Target

This inexpensive and invaluable piece of equipment is a must for anyone interested in improving their movement speed. Bruce Lee adopted this drill and used it regularly.

To construct a paper target, use an 8-by-11 sheet of paper. Tape one end of a piece of string to the top edge of the paper, and attach the other end to the ceiling or the top of a doorway. Adjust the string until the paper is at face height.

Practice shooting jabs at the paper. As the paper turns and twirls, try to anticipate when it will turn to face you again. When it does, immediately strike the paper. This will improve your visual reflexes too.

Do not stop the paper from twirling with your hands. Adapt to the paper, do not make the paper adapt to you. This will make the drill more challenging, which will elevate your speed and skill to a higher level.

For balanced speed development, alternate your leading hand while practicing the drill. Also, practice a variety of different punches and strikes. The constant use of this simple, inexpensive tool will improve your movement speed in less time than you thought possible.

The Paper Bag

For this drill, you will need a large paper bag. I've also used a cardboard box. You can still find these itcms in most grocery stores. The paper bag is a very useful tool for developing quick low kicks for competition. Effective low kicks to vital targets (knees, groin, etc.) can be critical to success in self-defense.

To practice your low kicks, simply set the paper bag or cardboard box on the floor and start kicking away! You can also attach a string to the bag and set it up so that it hangs from a ceiling or doorway.

Concentrate on *whipping* your kicks through the bag, as if it were an opponent's shin or knee.

Be sure to *snap* your kicks back in lightning-quick fashion.

You can spread out multiple bags and imagine being attacked by multiple assailants. Use your imagination to create additional scenarios.

Remember, you are developing extension and retraction speed, so concentrate intensely on moving from your ready position to kicking the bag over as fast as you can, and returning to the ready position as fast as possible.

Note: When training with the paper bag and the paper target, you should listen for the snapping sound of the paper as you strike it. If you are able to punch or kick a hole in the paper, you know that your movement speed is improving.

Repetitive Movement Speed

Repetitive movement speed is how quickly a strike can be thrown repeatedly with the same hand or foot. Not only are you concerned with how fast your punch or kick moves from point A to point B, you're also concerned with how fast you pull the punch or kick back from point B to point A, and extend it to point B again, and back to point A, and so on.

Repetitive movement speed gives you the ability to rapidly strike your opponent repeatedly with the same hand, foot, knee, elbow, etc. Although this type of speed is rarely applied in actual fighting, it should be developed because it will enhance your extension and retraction speed. It will also serve as an introduction to the muscle control necessary for developing overwhelming flow speed, the ultimate attribute for competition and self-defense.

To develop your repetitive movement speed, you can use the same training tools that you use for developing extension and retraction speed. Use the paper target and paper bag drills discussed earlier. The only difference is that now you will be using repetitive punches and kicks with the same hand or foot.

Start at two repetitive strikes and work your way up from there. Be sure to extend your arm or leg to near-full extension before re-cocking it. Also, be sure to cock your arm or leg completely before shooting it out again.

You could also practice repetitive speed drills in the air on the heavy bag, the speed bag, or the double-end bag. The key to developing repetitive speed is to concentrate on relaxing and firing rapidly.

Flow Speed

Flow speed is the ultimate attribute! Very few fighters possess this type of speed in abundance. Unfortunately, most fighters are hampering their own flow speed because they insist on clinging to rigid concepts and patterns.

I have seen trained martial artists with seemingly superior attributes get knocked out by novice martial artists. You may have heard stories of black belts getting their butts kicked by a street thug. How is it that an untrained adversary could defeat a highly trained martial artist?

One explanation is that a thug may possess superior innate attributes. A much more common explanation is this: *a thug is actually better trained than most martial artists for the setting in which you are most likely to meet him—the streets.*

You will not find a mugger at the local Karate school sweating profusely from a friendly sparring match. He is more comfortable in his own realm where he can prey on victims who are not as familiar with real fighting.

There is one vital rule of streetfighting that you must be aware of as you train for self-defense: *There are no rules in streetfighting!*

In most cases, a black belt should defeat an untrained streetfighter. But, if the black belt focuses too much on techniques, his mind becomes cluttered and his flow speed is hampered.

The average thug does not waste time thinking about techniques. He has a couple of techniques at his disposal, and he knows how to use them quickly, efficiently, and effectively. He has flow speed, even though his range of techniques is limited.

Once an attack starts, flow speed becomes critical for survival. Flow speed is a culmination of all the Speed Loop™ components, and it is a highly effective force. When we observe the great fighters of our time, we find few who possessed a high degree of flow speed. Those who did could easily overwhelm their opponents.

The legendary Bruce Lee possessed one of the highest levels of flow speed seen in the 20th century. He was known for his ability to overwhelm his opponent with speed. He could do this because very few of his contemporaries possessed high levels of flow speed.

Because of his superior flow speed, Bruce Lee could end a fight quickly. He could break down an opponent's defense with the overwhelming pressure of his fluid and relentless attack. The technique he used is called the straight blast.

In realistic combat situations, the best defense is a good offense. Superior flow speed will give you the deciding edge in a fight. If you can connect with the first good hit—and follow-up quickly and powerfully—you will usually emerge victorious. Do not pause or hesitate once you attack.

When you become totally aware of flow speed's impact on success in fighting, you will have taken a giant step forward in practical knowledge. Eventually, you will be able to simply observe people training or fighting and know if you are capable of defeating them with your flow.

Here are the drills that will maximize your flow speed.

Shadowfighting

This will greatly improve your flow speed when done correctly. You need good control of body mechanics to elevate your flow speed to a high level, and shadowfighting develops fundamental coordination.

Learn combinations that feel natural to you and practice executing them faster and faster. Then work on new combinations. Start slowly and work on speeding up as you become more relaxed and coordinated.

Do not be too concerned if you initially feel slow and awkward throwing various combinations. Keep training diligently and you will see consistent improvement. You are not practicing the combinations for specific application, but rather to enhance coordination and fluidity of movement, which will allow you to put much more pressure on an opponent.

Echo Drill

This drill is an excellent way to build the foundation for superior flow speed. The key to this drill is to move as quickly as possible from right-side attack to left-side attack and vice-versa. For instance: Throw a right jab-left jab-right jab-left jab. Or, throw a right front kick-left front kick-right front kick-left front kick. Keep pushing for more and more speed, but make sure you are relaxed and not straining. You can practice throwing alternating punches, kicks, elbows, or knees.

Sprinting

This is a drill that more martial artists should engage in for attribute enhancement. As small children, everyone who was physically capable ran sprints regularly. But, most adults can't remember the last time they ran a full-speed sprint.

Warning: You should always warm up and stretch before your sprint training. Otherwise, you risk injuring your muscles, tendons, or ligaments. Also, be certain to wear suitable footwear. You should consult your physician or local athletic footwear store on how to choose the best running shoes.

You can practice solo sprinting, or you can practice sprinting against a partner. You will benefit more if your partner is faster than you by a slight margin. Remember, you are trying to challenge and improve your physical skills.

Even though your partner may initially be faster, you should try your best to win. Use your imagination. Picture yourself outdistancing your partner.

Remember, your partner is probably also improving and may have started out at a higher level than you did, so don't get frustrated if you lose. Instead, you should focus on being better than you were yesterday.

When sprinting solo, you can race against the clock. Use a stopwatch or simply count the seconds using any watch. Timing yourself gives you a goal to shoot for, as well as tangible proof of your improvement.

You can accelerate your speed improvement by wearing a weighted vest when sprinting. If the weather or conditions outside are not suitable, you can find an indoor track for sprinting. Or, you can try running in place as fast as you can.

Sprinting speed is similar to flow speed in martial arts. When sprinting, you are trying to move as fast as you can while relaxing your body and detaching your mind. Also, you are developing that intimate "feel" for the optimum tension level and learning to maintain it during rapid movement.

Sparring

When done realistically, sparring helps develop flow speed. You can practice sparring with your partner at half-speed in order to develop your basic sense of flowing. As your reflexes and speed improve, you should speed up the action until you are eventually ready for full-speed contact sparring with protective gear. Concentrate on exploding your attack when you sense the optimal attack moment. Once the flow begins, keep it going until one of you concedes.

Although full-contact sparring is not actual combat, it will familiarize you with the ranges, rhythm, contact, adrenaline rush, and flow of combat. But, keep in mind that you cannot use the most effective self-defense techniques (eye gouging, biting, groin strikes, throat strikes, face claws, and joint breaks) when sparring. You can practice developing these more vicious techniques for self-defense.

Audible Rhythm Hitting

You have learned how to use visualization to help develop your speed. Audible rhythm hitting is another secret tool you can use to enhance any speed drill.

Here is how it works: If you are shadowfighting and you want to throw a lightning-quick three-punch combination, you would first "sound off" the three strikes at the speed and pace you want them to be. Now, you should actually throw the combination at the same speed and pace of the sounds. You can use any sound you want.

Let's suppose you want to throw lightning-quick kicks: a right-side kick, a left-side kick, another right-side kick, and one more left-side kick. That's four kicks altogether. Before actually kicking, you would sound the kicks off at the speed and pace you want to throw them. Then, relax and fire the four kicks at that desired speed and pace.

You will notice many people unconsciously using this principle when training, or fighting. Boxers use this principle when hitting the focus pads and the heavy bag. Even children use this principle when they imitate their martial arts heroes.

Coupled with visualization, self-hypnosis, and progressively more challenging drills, audible rhythm hitting will help maximize your movement speed in the shortest possible time.

Chapter 8

Alteration Speed

Most fighters overlook alteration speed. But, if you are a serious speed student, you will develop this valuable safeguard.

Alteration speed involves the ability to quickly change directions in the midst of movement. Essentially, it involves control of balance and inertia.

Alteration speed is invaluable during those moments when an opponent offsets your timing or precision and you find yourself on the defensive end of a ferocious attack. Alteration speed also enhances your speed hampering ability by making it easier to break your opponent's rhythm, because you are able to control your own rhythm more effectively.

With good alteration speed, you can initiate an attack, perceive the opponent's counter, alter your movement accordingly, and effectively counter the opponent's original counterattack. When two highly skilled fighters face off, this complete exchange can take place in a split second.

Once you have attained advanced levels of alteration speed, you will be able to stop instantaneously, in the flow of movement, as if you have run into an invisible brick wall (lucky for you, or that invisible brick wall could be a very visible fist).

As all great fighters know, the best time to attack is when the opponent is initiating an attack. This concept can be carried out by what is commonly referred to as the stop-hit. Stop-hitting is an essential basic skill for successful counter-fighting. Alteration speed will help you avoid becoming a victim of the stop-hit and other counter-attacks.

Dynamic Balance

Dynamic balance is simply the ability to throw your center of gravity beyond the base of support, chase it, and never let it get away.

To instantly improve your balance, follow these guidelines:

1. Keep your center of gravity low.
2. Keep your feet shoulder-width apart.
3. Keep your weight on the balls of the feet.
4. Keep your knees slightly bent at all times.

Many stances found in the martial arts are unrealistic for real combat. They are not active and natural. As a guide, you should avoid stances that feel stiff, weak, rigid, or uncomfortable. We are not tigers, snakes, eagles, or butterflies. We are humans. We have to discover the best fighting positions for our particular design. It is imperative that you learn to adapt and maintain a dynamic fighting position that will facilitate explosive movements.

Kinesthetic Perception

Maintaining the optimum fighting position requires a high level of kinesthetic perception. This is the faculty that allows you to feel variation in muscle contraction and relaxation. The only way to develop this faculty is to place the body in different positions and become highly sensitive to how tense or relaxed you feel in these positions.

You are looking for the position that makes you feel most relaxed and will allow you to explode in a split second. As a starting point, use a boxer's stance. You can try lowering your head, raising your lead hand, dropping your shoulder slightly, turning your knees in slightly, etc. You goal is to achieve a relaxed and natural feeling of alertness in your body.

Once you have attained a feeling of relaxation in your basic fighting position, you can use it as a constant guide to your body as it moves. You want to progress from static kinesthetic perception to dynamic kinesthetic perception.

Caution: Your fighting position will be constantly changing depending on the circumstances of each encounter. You must be prepared to make quick adjustments if you want to succeed in competition and self-defense.

Dynamic Balance Drills

The following drills will develop your dynamic kinesthetic perception. With consistent training, you will instinctively and consistently position your body in a way that permits maximum results with minimal effort.

Blind Shadowfighting

If you practice blind shadowfighting regularly, you will quickly notice an improvement in your dynamic balance.

Start by finding an open area where you will not injure yourself. Close your eyes. Assume your fighting position. Now, visualize a menacing opponent in front of you. Imagine him attacking you. You respond with the perfect counter and the flow keeps going. Throw knees and kicks to challenge your balance skills. Try fighting multiple opponents at one time. Use your imagination to get yourself into a fighting frame of mind.

Blind Rope Skipping

This ancient exercise is even more challenging when done with your eyes closed. Blind rope skipping will dramatically improve your dynamic balance. It will also improve agility, coordination, and stamina.

Caution: Make sure your skipping area is free of objects that could injure you, in case you drift slightly while skipping with your eyes closed. It is okay to open your eyes periodically to see where you are.

Begin with a slow and simple skipping routine. You can skip rope to music to make it more enjoyable. Relax and concentrate on keeping your balance.

Once you are comfortable with blind rope skipping, you can increase the difficulty by doing crossovers or double turns. Consider purchasing a book, video, or DVD on jumping rope to learn routines that will continue to challenge your dynamic balance.

Gymnastics and Tumbling

This sport is great for developing a foundation for dynamic balance. It will help you overcome the fear of being airborne. Once you overcome this fear, you will notice the improvement in your kinesthetic perception when you are grounded. I suggest you find a competent instructor and learn the basic moves and tumbles. Your goal is to overcome fear and tension when placing your body in unfamiliar positions.

Blind Wrestling

This is an advanced dynamic balance drill. With both you and your partner blindfolded, start by "locking up" each other's arms. Count to three—and go for it! Initially, you will find it difficult to remain relaxed when your partner tries to sweep or slam you. But, concentrate on maintaining a relaxed body and it will eventually become a habit.

Since you will need to stick to your partner, your tactile reflexes will also receive a good workout from this drill. This rigorous drill will also challenge other components of the Speed Loop™.

Caution: Practice blind wrestling in an open area with a suitable surface, so you and your partner can avoid injury. Proceed with caution and stop if you or your partner becomes fatigued.

Static Balance

In addition to the dynamic balance drills, you should practice static balance drills. An example would be raising one leg in the air and holding it in place for as long as you can. Close your eyes to increase the difficulty of this drill.

Static balance drills are useful if you find that the dynamic drills are initially too difficult. It is okay to start at a point that is comfortable for you. Just be sure to consistently challenge yourself to improve.

Chapter 9

Speed Hampering

Speed hampering is anything that you do to effectively slow down the opponent's reaction time to your attacks. Reaction time is the time gap between a stimulus and the response. Skill in speed hampering can help compensate for what you may lack in movement speed.

> **Secret:** If you double your movement speed, halve your reaction time, and double your opponent's reaction time, you will have effectively tripled your actual speed!

As a speed student, you should commit to becoming proficient at speed hampering. Speed hampering skill will give you an edge in speed that will cause unenlightened opponents to feel as if you are completely dictating the fight with superior reflexes. Your opponent's confidence can be deflated very quickly if he or she feels helpless against your attacks.

Speed hampering is an effective way to take over a fight on the psychological level, which nearly always ensures a swift victory. Once you have the opponent's mind, the body will follow!

The basic principle of speed hampering is to distract the opponent's mind long enough to launch an effective attack. A split-second distraction is all you should need to initiate your flow successfully.

You must always remain acutely aware of any lull in the opponent's concentration. At that split second, you must react instantly and decisively, making absolutely certain that the opponent never gets a chance to recover from a lapse in focus, because he or she is frantically trying to halt your relentless attack.

Reaction Time

Total reaction time is determined by three factors:

1. The time required for the stimulus to reach the brain
2. The time required for the brain to relay the impulse through the proper nerve fibers to the correct muscles
3. The time required for the muscles to start and complete the action demanded of them

People's reaction times are longer under the following conditions:

1. When they first initiate a movement
2. When they are in the midst of movement
3. When they are mentally distracted
4. When they are physically tired
5. When they are overly emotional

You should launch your attack when you catch your opponent in one of these vulnerable situations. It is essential that you time your attack for the right moment physically and psychologically, when the opponent cannot avoid being caught off guard. As you train to react to these moments, your offensive success rate will consistently improve.

As a superior fighter, you must sense rather than observe your chance to attack. In other words, you should be all over the opponent before *you* even realize what happened! That's the power of the flow on automatic pilot.

There are specific ways you can increase your opponent's reaction time by inducing a vulnerable condition. You could shout loudly, stomp your feet, gaze insanely, act simple-minded, smile, slobber, or even whisper. It's simply a matter of selecting the right deception at the right time. That is the key.

Timing

To effectively hamper the opponent, you must develop the attribute of good timing. In fighting, timing is the art of successfully launching an attack when it will connect with maximum velocity and impact. In the case of strikes, this is when the opponent is coming forward.

The best way to begin developing a sense of timing is to work with the double-end bag. This tool is absolutely invaluable. With practice, your timing and distance skills will reach a level where you can consistently hit the elusive bag with jabs, kicks, elbows, and head butts.

You can improve your timing by training with focus gloves. The key to developing good timing with the focus gloves is to solicit the help of a skilled manipulator to hold them.

Feinting

Feinting is a characteristic of the expert fighter. It requires using the eyes, arms, legs, and every other part of the body in a concerted effort to get a reaction from the opponent. The purpose of feinting is to create an opening that will improve the chances of success when launching an attack.

Feinting creates momentary openings. To take advantage of these openings, you must have quick reflexes. An advanced speed student knows what openings will result before they feint, and they make use of that knowledge by initiating their attack before the opening actually occurs.

The essential elements of good feinting are creativity, deception, rhythm, quickness, and precision. You must be careful not to feint unnecessarily because it increases your risk of being attacked by your opponent.

Do not get carried away with feints. Do not feint excessively for the sake of trying to embarrass or ridicule an opponent. Strive to be simple, efficient, and direct in your strategy to defeat an opponent.

The speed and quantity of your feints should be adjusted to the opponent's speed and rhythm. A feint that is executed too quickly on a slower opponent will not get a reaction in time. You can use a faster feint to hamper and trap an opponent who possesses superior movement speed.

You can practice feinting while using different tools, such as the heavy bag, double-end bag, and focus gloves. Of course, you should practice feinting while sparring. When two fighters with equal attributes face each other, the one with superior strategy and hampering skill will emerge victorious.

Stop-Hitting

A stop-hit is a timed hit made against the opponent at the same time they are launching an attack. In the Filipino martial arts, it is called "de-fanging the snake" and includes stop-hits directed at the arms, legs, and body as well as the head. Stop-hitting is an advanced form of speed hampering that requires a shift in thinking for most fighters who may be accustomed to evading or blocking an attack. The psychological benefit of stop-hitting is that it gets you into the habit of attacking when you are attacked, instead of defending when you are attacked. Stop-hitting is not passive, it is active! The key to developing intimidating stop-hitting skill in your training is to focus on hitting your opponent at every opportunity.

Successful stop-hitting requires sharp reflexes and intense concentration. You must anticipate and intercept the intended attack with skilled timing and precision. A successful stop-hit is made possible by keen visual, auditory, and tactile reflexes. Your timing, distance, and accuracy must be exact when executing the stop-hit. If your stop-hit fails, you will miss your target and possibly end up in the opponent's direct line of attack.

You should use the stop-hit when the opponent is stepping forward. You want your opponent to commit so as to lose the ability to change directions and defend against attack. To further hamper your opponent, you should move forward when executing the stop-hit.

Familiarity with the angles of fighting will help you become more skilled at stop-hitting. You can learn these angles from boxing and the Filipino martial arts. As a speed student, you should train yourself to be constantly prepared to stop-hit an opponent during any phase of a fight. Learn to use the stop-hit with great speed, power, and accuracy from every possible angle.

The ability to effectively stop-hit an opponent in a real fight is an invaluable yet advanced skill. Your ability to stop-hit can save you when you are surprised by an attack and want to disrupt the opponent's flow.

Your ability to execute effective stop-hits can pacify an opponent's offense. Your opponent will move forward cautiously after you show you can quickly inflict pain.

Chapter 10

Supplemental Speed Training

This chapter was included as a bonus to help you maximize your speed after you have developed the basic components of your Speed Loop™.

The basic building block of any skilled physical performance is physical fitness. Just as there are components of speed, there are also components of physical fitness. The three basic components of physical fitness are stamina, strength, and flexibility. When properly developed, these three fundamental attributes will improve any skilled physical performance.

In order to become the best possible fighter, you must develop a high level of fundamental physical fitness. High levels of physical fitness will dramatically enhance your skilled attributes such as speed, power, accuracy, timing, and agility. This is the hallmark of highly effective martial artists. Their superior fitness and attributes allow them to easily transcend styles and quickly integrate new concepts into their mixed martial arts repertoire.

You would be wise to model the legendary fighters by devoting the bulk of your training time to improving fitness and attributes. To make rapid progress, you have to invest your time effectively. Superior fitness and attributes are the foundation for success in martial arts. Don't fall into the trap of spending too much time on sophisticated techniques and not enough time on specialized drills and conditioning.

Learn to maximize your strengths and minimize your weaknesses. The best way to minimize weaknesses is by nurturing and developing them, not by ignoring them. In the heat of battle, your opponent will not ignore your weaknesses. Rather, your opponent will exploit them. It is better to face the reality of your shortcomings in training, than to face that reality in the midst of battle.

Strength Training

Martial artists, boxers, and athletes in general have adopted weight lifting as part of their regular training. It was once thought that lifting weights would make you slow, and compromise your skill and coordination. That notion, as many great athletes have repeatedly shown, has been completely invalidated.

All of today's top fighters supplement their training with weights, and as a result, today's fighters are stronger and faster than ever before.

Weight training tones the muscles, which increases their ability to contract quickly. When using weights, you have to train with a specific purpose in mind if you want to achieve useful results.

Although, there are many gadgets on the market that claim to be superior to free weights, the truth of the matter is that none of these gadgets will improve your strength and speed faster or more effectively than free weights. What Olympic-level weight lifter have you heard of who trained by using a machine purchased from a television infomercial?

Free weights force you to balance the weight of the barbell or dumbbells. The extra balancing effort exerted by your muscles forces them to adapt and respond by growing stronger more quickly.

> **Note**: High quality machines that offer safe and effective resistance can also be very useful for strength training.

Strength training can improve every attribute if applied correctly. To get started, you should invest in quality resistance equipment, or join a health club that has quality resistance equipment.

Caution: To help ensure safety and effectiveness, I strongly recommend having a certified trainer help you set up your strength-training program.

Secret: John Jesse authored the finest book on strength training and conditioning I have ever read. It is titled *Wrestling Physical Conditioning Encyclopedia.* The book is currently out of print, but you can visit us at FitnessLifestyle.com to find out how you can get a copy. If you want to achieve exceptional physical fitness, you should have this book.

Flexibility Training

The more flexible you are, the more relaxed your muscles will be, and the faster you can move without risking injury. A fighter who is more flexible has more body control, which is essential to initiation speed and movement speed.

Caution: Always warm up prior to stretching. You can walk, ride a bike, or do some slow shadowfighting. The whole idea is to raise your body temperature and warm up your muscles. Warm muscles stretch better than cold muscles.

There are two basic types of stretching, dynamic and static. To improve your flexibility rapidly with minimum injury, you should adhere to a program of static stretching. Static stretching will allow you to progressively improve your flexibility.

Everyone has different needs when it comes to stretching. Get to know which of your joints are loose and supple, and which are tight and less supple. You can make more effective use of your time by concentrating on the exercises that will increase the flexibility of the joints that need it most.

There are many factors that determine your flexibility: genetics, gender, training program, age, fitness level, diet, and muscle tone, just to name a few. The key is to focus your time and energy on those factors that you can influence. Never waste your valuable time on factors you clearly have no control over. Accept them and move on!

Stamina Training

Aerobics are used to strengthen the most important muscle: the heart. By increasing your stamina level, you will be able to flow for longer periods of time.

Contrary to what some advertisements claim, most fights will require more than one "killer" move. Often, stamina will be the limiting factor of your fighting capability. Once you are tired, speed and everything else goes out the window.

Without endurance, all of your other attributes are severely limited. When you are fatigued, you are weaker, slower, more careless, and less precise in your thoughts and actions.

Endurance and stamina training should be the number one priority on every superior fighter's training schedule, regardless of style.

Endurance training can be either aerobic (with oxygen), or anaerobic (without oxygen). Although fighting is almost purely anaerobic, you should use cardiovascular exercise in the form of aerobics as the foundation of your endurance training. You should gradually insert anaerobic bursts or high-speed intervals into your training. The bursts will improve your overall aerobic capacity. They will also simulate the bursts of energy necessary to overwhelm an opponent during a fight.

To get adequate aerobic exercise, physiologists tell us that we should raise our pulse to target zone for 20 to 30 minutes, and that we should do this at least 3 times a week. You can find your target zone by subtracting your age from 220.

Then multiply the difference by 0.6 to get your target low, and by 0.8 to get your target high.

The two figures that you come up with will represent your target range. You are advised to keep your pulse within this range when exercising aerobically.

A commonly used barometer of whether you are exercising aerobically or anaerobically is the "talk test." If you can carry on a normal conversation without much effort, you are doing aerobics. If you can barely get out a word, or if you are holding your breath, you are doing anaerobics.

It is important to insert high-speed intervals into your attribute-training sessions. This will help you develop the anaerobic endurance that is essential for developing a highly effective flow. As you begin implementing anaerobics, you will experience an uncomfortable ache in your muscles. The goal is to make this feeling of discomfort so familiar that it becomes an ally in competition or self-defense.

Well-trained wrestlers and grapplers have high levels of anaerobic endurance. I have watched marathon runners end up completely out of gas after grappling for a couple of rounds. Marathoners have high levels of aerobic endurance. They do not necessarily have the high levels of anaerobic endurance found in wrestlers and grapplers.

To develop your anaerobic endurance fast, you should practice grappling with someone who has more strength and stamina than you have.

Caution: Always check with your physician prior to starting any cardiovascular exercise program.

The Balanced Diet

As a speed student, you want to feel your best in order to get the most out of your training. Good basic health is a prerequisite to high levels of fitness.

A leaner athlete is a faster athlete. Excessive body fat will hinder your speed. You should strive to achieve low levels of body fat through your training and diet.

Do not become fanatical with losing every ounce of body fat. Some body fat is necessary for good health and adequate energy levels.

You must also take genetics into account. Some people are meant to be leaner than others. Just do what you can to achieve your optimum level of body fat. This is the level at which you feel your quickest.

Your diet should be built on common sense. For starters, avoid foods that are high in saturated fat, trans fat, hydrogenated oils, salt (sodium), high calories, and refined sugar. You can eat these types of foods occasionally. The key is to avoid making these types of foods the foundation of your daily diet. The foods at the foundation of your diet should be high in fiber, protein, vitamins, minerals, and complex carbohydrates.

Try to eat something from all food groups. Strive to increase your consumption of water, fruits and vegetables. Strive to decrease your consumption of junk food and fast foods. This will ensure that you are getting all of the proper nutrients. Try to avoid becoming fanatical about your diet. Instead, keep it simple and focus on stressing variety in your daily meals, while staying aware of what is healthy and what is not. Learn how to substitute healthy alternatives for less-healthy foods. Continue to improve your diet by educating yourself on how to make healthy eating choices, like how to shop for and prepare healthy foods, and how to eat healthy when dining out.

Drink plenty of pure water every day. It is the second most important component of health, after adequate rest. Substitute fresh water in place of sodas and artificial juices. This alone can help you shed unwanted pounds.

It is okay to drink water during your workouts. I recommend distilled water. You can't verify the source of spring water because everyone is selling it. I've tasted spring water that is worse than tap water. With distilled water, at least I know it was boiled and it offers the best chance of purity.

The best way to evaluate a food is to be acutely aware of how it affects you physically and mentally. Do you feel sluggish? Is your stomach upset? Are you more energetic? Is your concentration improved? On a daily basis, you must decide which foods will fuel your body. The results of your decisions will be clearly evident in how you look and feel.

Nutritional Supplements

Many martial artists use nutritional supplements to help maintain their basic health and fitness. Despite the best intentions to eat a well-balanced diet every day, the vast majority of people will fall short. At a minimum, nutritional supplements offer insurance against nutritional deficiency. Optimally, nutritional supplements can improve function and performance.

Ideally, you should take a vitamin deficiency test to see which vitamins are lacking in your daily diet. You can then take the vitamins you need to makeup for the deficiency. This test will also prevent you from spending money on supplements you don't need.

Look in your local phone book under nutritionist. If you cannot locate a nutritionist, ask your personal physician if they can test you, or refer you to someone who can.

I will avoid recommending a particular brand of vitamins. I will just say that a good multivitamin that includes all of the necessary daily nutrients is a good start. You can try additional products to see if they enhance your health and fitness, but you should consult your physician.

To make sure your reflexes are functioning at their peak, it is important to have a sufficient supply of all B-vitamins. They aid in converting carbohydrates into glucose, and are necessary for the normal functioning of the nervous system.

Because nutritional supplements can be expensive and sometimes dangerous, you should be wary of outlandish or unproven claims about benefits and results. If you have questions about a supplement, talk to a qualified health care professional.

Training Log

The training log is an indispensable tool for the superior fighter. With the help of a training log, you can minimize wasteful actions and maximize results. An effective training log system will help you progress faster.

What you actually record in your training log is up to you. It depends on what is important or which components of the Speed Loop™ you are concentrating on developing.

Some of the things I have listed in my training log include: date, training tool, duration, speed component, training partners, body tools or weapons emphasized, progress notes, and pertinent comments (suggestions for improvement, general observations, etc.)

The purpose of your training log is to help you get better. Period. You can use a paper log or an electronic log. Either way, you should use it to track and encourage your progress. In addition to using the log consistently, you must be honest and accurate when recording your workouts.

To get the most out of your training, review your training log before and after each workout. As you do this, imagine yourself improving the Speed Loop™ components you are focused on developing. You will discover that using a training log accelerates your progress toward maximum speed development.

Conclusion

Congratulations!

You have completed the study of Speed Training for Martial Arts. As you start applying this information, you will be delighted by the transformation in your total speed and fighting ability.

Reading this guide will not turn you into the greatest fighter on earth. However, if you apply the information as instructed, you will significantly improve your martial arts speed for competition and self-defense. This guide is guaranteed to improve your speed and help you become the best martial artist you can be.

By covering one specific attribute, speed, in great detail, my mission is to keep this guide distinguished and highly regarded. My focus will always be on maintaining the highest standard of quality by offering specialized knowledge that is innovative, adaptable, and highly effective.

When your speed and reflexes start improving, please send me an e-mail (by contacting my publisher at kevin.jonesy@gmail.com) and let me know about your accomplishments. My hope is that this guide makes a positive contribution to your total personal growth.

J. Barnes

Fitness Lifestyle Commitment

Thank you for purchasing *Speed Training for Martial Arts and MMA*. With each publication, our goal is to provide solutions that are simple, effective, and affordable.

We hope that you continue to look to us, to help you improve in the face of life's constant challenges. We would love to hear your comments, suggestions, and ideas.

Healthy Wishes,

Kevin J. Jones

C.E.O. and Publisher

kevin.jonesy@gmail.com

Index

A

adaptation speed, 69-82
   Number Call, 76
adrenaline, 41-45, 109, 122
Advanced Sound trigger, 65
aerobic, 149-152
Aikido, 58
alteration speed, 125-132
anaerobic, 149-152
ankle weights, 104-106
anticipation skill, 49-54
   Focus Glove Snatch, 53, 97
   Pet Snatch, 52
   Traffic Light, 51
   TV Response, 50
   Video games, 52
applied speed, 24-26, 83
audible rhythm hitting, 123-124
auditory reflexes, 65-69, 109
   Advanced Sound Trigger, 65
   Basic Sound Trigger, 64
   Intermediate Sound Trigger, 65
   Solo Sound Trigger, 66

B

Basic Sound Trigger, 64
blink control, 35-38
   Blink Challenge, 36
Book Drop, 98-100

C

C.C.S. Principle, 26-27
Chi, *See* Ki
Combat Common Sense, 26-27
cycling, 74

D

D.S.P., 49
diet, 149, 152-155
Double Hand Sensitivity Drill, 60
dynamic balance, 126-129
Dynamic Balance Drills, 129
   Blind Rope Skipping, 130
   Blind Shadowfighting, 120
   Blind wrestling, 131-132
   Gymnastics & Tumbling, 131

E

Echo Drill, 119
environmental training, 82-85, 89,
escrima sticks, 70, 72
E.S.P., *See* Sixth Sense
explosiveness, 58, 79, 87, 98-103
extension speed, 109-110
Eye Exercises, 31-35
   Circular Eye Stretch, 33
   Eye Massage, 34
   Eye Squeeze, 34
   Lateral Eye Stretch, 32
   Vertical Eye Stretch, 32

F

feinting, 54, 137-139
Filipino Martial Arts, 70-71, 139-140

flexibility training, 148-149
flow speed, 114-122
Focus Glove Snatch, 53, 97 focus gloves, 74-76,
100, 137, 139
focus point, 38, 55, 95

G
grappling, 55-59, 61, 152
   Blind Grappling, 61

H
heavy bag, 75,101-102, 115, 123, 138

I
inch training, 100
initiation speed, 87-88, 91, 97-99, 107, 148
Intermediate Sound trigger, 65
Isolation Principle, 28, 109,
isolation training, 28

J
Judo, 58
Jujitsu, 58

K
Kali, 58
Ki, 42-43
kinesthetic perception, 89, 127-131

L
Lee, Bruce. 111, 117

Made in the USA
Lexington, KY
07 September 2012